Royal College of Physicians
History and Heritage Series

GW00730257

Denys Lasdun's
Royal College of Physicians
A monumental act of faith

Barnabas Calder

2008

Royal College
of Physicians
Setting higher medical standards

Acknowledgements

Commissioned and edited by Emma Shepley, Curator,
Royal College of Physicians.

We would like to thank Dr Mark Crinson and Dr Alan Powers for their
suggestions on the text, Zoe Brealey for her research assistance with the
text, and Sir Richard Thompson, College Treasurer, for his support.

History and Heritage Series Editorial Board

Dr Andrew Hilson (Harveian Librarian), Professor Alastair Compston and
Sir Christopher Booth.

The Royal College of Physicians

The Royal College of Physicians plays a leading role in the delivery of high
quality patient care by setting standards of medical practice and promoting
clinical excellence. We provide physicians in the United Kingdom and
overseas with education, training and support throughout their careers.
As an independent body representing over 20,000 Fellows and Members
worldwide, we advise and work with government, the public, patients and
other professions to improve health and healthcare.

Copyright

All rights reserved. No part of this publication may be reproduced in any
form (including photocopying or storing it in any medium by electronic
means and whether or not transiently or incidentally to some other use of
this publication) without the written permission of the copyright owner.
Applications for the copyright owner's written permission to reproduce any
part of this publication should be addressed to the publisher.

The Royal College of Physicians has made every reasonable effort to
contact and acknowledge copyright owners of all images in this publication
and wishes to be informed by any copyright owners who are not properly
identified and acknowledged so that we may make any necessary
corrections in future editions. To contact us, email:
heritage@rcplondon.ac.uk

Copyright © 2008 Royal College of Physicians

ISBN 978-1-86016-328-9

Royal College of Physicians of London

11 St Andrews Place, London NW1 4LE

www.rcplondon.ac.uk

Registered Charity No 210508

Designed and typeset by WLG Design Limited
Printed by The Lavenham Press Ltd, Suffolk

Contents

View of the College from the south side garden

'It is a privilege to work on a daily basis in one of the finest 20th-century buildings in London.'

Foreword

It is a privilege to work on a daily basis in one of the finest 20th-century buildings in London. Sir Denys Lasdun's creation has been an inspiration to the College since its opening in 1964 and we owe a debt of gratitude to the then President, Robert Platt, for his prescience in commissioning an innovative modern building to house one of the most historic institutions in England. Today the building works for the College directly in many ways: as the headquarters of our work setting standards in clinical practice, education and training for physicians; as a world-class venue for conferences and events; and as the setting for the College's historic collections of portraits, silver, archives and the treasures of the Dorchester Library. It remains an astonishing building over forty years after its completion, not least in its flexibility in meeting the challenges of changing College functions while retaining its original character.

While initially nearly all visitors would have been physicians and those connected to medicine, today we are proud to throw open our doors to the public for architectural visits and on occasions such as London Open House so that they too can enter the galleried Marble Hall, designed by Lasdun as the College's inner sanctum, and experience for themselves this extraordinary building. This publication reveals the complexity and above all, the feats of engineering with which Lasdun skilfully amalgamated our traditions with his modernity, and it is a fascinating story.

Ian Gilmore
President, Royal College of Physicians

Sir Denys Lasdun (1914–2001)

Denys Lasdun studied at the Architectural Association where he became a firm adherent of the modern movement. Le Corbusier's *Vers une Architecture* was to remain an influence on him all his life. In 1937 Lasdun worked for Wells Coates (1895–1958), and then with Tecton – the progressive architectural group formed by Berthold Lubetkin (1901–1990), designer of the Highpoint flats in Highgate and the London Zoo penguin pool.

Lasdun established his independent reputation after the war with a delightful school in Paddington, innovative council housing in Bethnal Green, and a graceful block of flats in St James's Place, overlooking Green Park. At Green Park and at the Royal College of Physicians he made unequivocally modern buildings harmonise with classical neighbours by careful choice of materials and an underlying sympathy for the proportions and principles of classicism.

In 1959 Lasdun established Denys Lasdun & Partners, winning numerous prestigious commissions including the new University of East Anglia in Norwich, and the National Theatre on London's South Bank. The latter was to become the defining building of Lasdun's career. From the start the National Theatre has divided opinion between those who dislike its grey colour and its sober architecture, and those who love the wood-marks in its concrete and the dramatic spaces of its foyers.

Lasdun defended many aspects of the modern movement when both its beliefs and aesthetics were facing severe criticism. His own massive and uncompromising concrete and glass structures often made him the object of attacks, the Prince of Wales famously declaring in 1988 that the National Theatre was 'a clever way of building a nuclear power station in the middle of London without anyone objecting'.

Lasdun did receive much support and recognition; knighted in 1976 and made a member of the Order of the Companions of Honour in 1995, he was awarded the RIBA Royal Gold Medal for architecture in 1977. Elected to the Royal Academy in 1991, in 1997 the Academy honoured him with a retrospective exhibition and its architect members have rallied to defend Lasdun's monumental legacy.

Introduction

When Denys was approached as a possible architect for the new building of the Royal College of Physicians, he and I went to Trafalgar Square to look at their headquarters and check out the ambience. Denys was not too hopeful, given that the College was then housed in Smirke's classical building in Pall Mall East. He knew that as a committed modernist he would be ruled out if they wanted another 'traditional' building. When, at his subsequent interview, one of the selection committee looked out of the window and asked, pointing to Herbert Baker's grandiose classical South Africa House, if he would build like that, he answered with an unequivocal 'No'. He was later assured that the College was already committed to a modern building and he was duly appointed as their architect.

... when one of the selection committee looked out of the window and asked, pointing to Herbert Baker's grandiose classical South Africa House, if he would build like that, he answered with an unequivocal 'No'.

There followed an intense dialogue with the Building Committee in which Denys discovered the College's needs, functions, roles and rituals, together with their aspirations for the future. While discussing the more prosaic requirements, the dialogue ended in what became a memorable phrase for Denys, 'and the usual staircase'. As is evident, this 'staircase' became the architectural heart of the building. From then on the Building Committee gave Denys their unswerving support in spite of any private doubts some members may have held. In his words 'they left him alone to get on with the design'.

They had been the perfect committee to work with which led him to the theory that 'Clients get the buildings they deserve'. In the case of RCP – which was always how the 'job' was referred to in his office and at home – the College got one of the best buildings he designed. He never ceased to be impressed by the breadth of knowledge and interests, outside of their profession,

Left **Sir Denys Lasdun by Anthony Crickmay** (© V&A Images/Victoria and Albert Museum)

which so many physicians had, including in some cases a wide knowledge of the arts. The President, Robert Platt, was a fine cellist and was deeply concerned that the acoustics in the Dorchester Library should be of a high order since he was planning to hold recitals and chamber music concerts in that room. Dr Alistair Hunter, Dean of St George's Hospital Medical School, had an exceptional collection of modern art, which he bequeathed to the Fitzwilliam Museum. Apart from being a staunch supporter of Denys, he was one of the most articulate men on the visual arts whom either of us ever met, and became a good friend. Dr Richard Bomford, the Treasurer, was another Fellow who gave invaluable counsel to Denys.

Denys treasured his continuing relationship with the College. He was proud to have been made an Honorary Fellow and honoured to have been presented with a miniature version of the College's silver caduceus – a gift awarded to only a handful of College friends and benefactors. He was deeply touched by the beautiful engraved glasses with which he was presented on his eightieth birthday, together with the dinner party which was given for him. He was also grateful for the pristine condition in which the College has always been maintained.

My family and I were deeply appreciative to have been allowed to hold his Memorial Service in the building. I am also extremely touched that the College have extended their friendship to myself since Denys's death by making me a Friend of the College. In short, the relationship with the College has been an entirely enriching experience for our family for which we are enormously grateful.

Susan Lasdun

The story of Lasdun's building

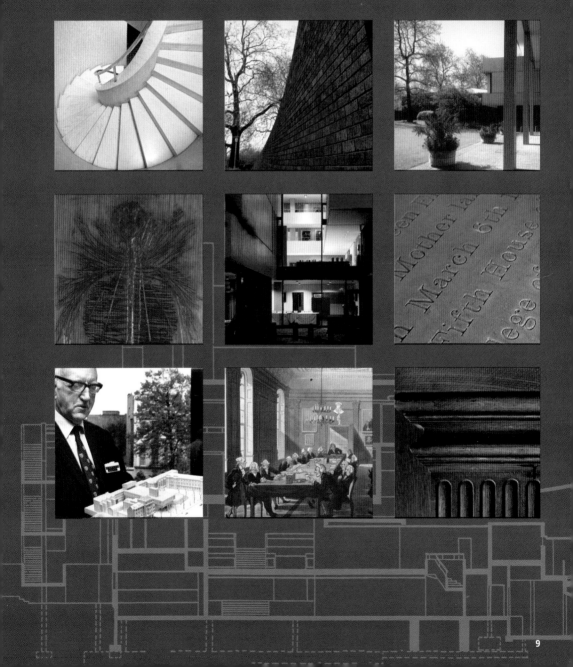

Choosing Mr Lasdun

The Royal College of Physicians was changing. After his uncompromising refusal at interview to build a traditionally classical building, Denys Lasdun expected to be rejected as their architect, but he did not know about the new spirit which was spreading in the College. The President, Robert (later Lord) Platt (1900–78), had come in just the previous year with a determination to modernise the institution. His predecessor, Dr Walter Russell Brain, 1st Baron Brain, had believed that the College had no business involving itself in the private affairs of the population, and had consequently discouraged medical pronouncements on public health. Platt felt that such a learned body had a duty to tell people if they were making themselves ill, and a few years later, on 7 March 1962, he was to hold the first ever press conference of the Royal College of Physicians. This press conference announced the results of the College's radical report, *Smoking and health*. A new era had begun in which the College would conduct and publicise studies on health questions that affected the whole nation.

When the Canadian government expressed a wish to expand into the parts of their shared building in Trafalgar Square previously occupied by the College, Platt saw a chance to express this modernising spirit in built form. Moving to new premises would permit him to update the institution, and could provide the necessary offices and room for lectures to make the College an effective participant in professional and national discussions on medical science and health policy. The physicians would move from a building which was essentially a gentleman's club to strikingly modern new premises with the latest facilities.

St Andrews Place by John Nash facing the College site and Regent's Park

Portrait of President Robert Platt by Merlyn Evans, 1963

John Summerson (1904–92), curator of Sir John Soane's Museum and a respected expert on architecture, was consulted by the physicians. He agreed that they must choose a modern architect, and accept a modern building. He also suggested Lasdun as a possible candidate.[1] The physicians, armed with photographs of Lasdun's work, and presumably impressed by his authoritative and serious interview performance, chose him; he was offered the position of architect for the new building on 17 October 1958.[2]

The architect recognised that 'Robert Platt was a visionary, and he knew he had to build for tomorrow and not for yesterday'.[3] However, he felt that a modernist building had been commissioned by the majority of the physicians 'in a mixed spirit of trepidation and unenthusiasm'.[4] The risk that the College felt it was taking is clear in the minute of a speech given by the President himself to the governing body – note the use of the word 'nevertheless':

> 'The building committee in choosing Mr. Denys Lasdun had for its architect a man who was uncompromising in his refusal to build anything that was a mere imitation of something which had been done better in the past. Nevertheless, he had assured the President personally that he could design a building of grace, dignity and charm that would be suitable for the College functions and traditions.'[5]

The extent to which the building could have turned out differently if the College had chosen a more traditional solution is clear from the Royal College of Obstetricians and Gynaecologists building, which opened in 1960 on the other side of Regent's Park. There Louis de Soissons produced a building in a modernised classical architecture indubitably sensitive to the surrounding Nash terraces, but equally clearly less exciting and less architecturally admired than Lasdun's College.

This part of the book will look at the development of the College design and at its reception. First, 'Architect and client' will discuss the distinctive manner in which Lasdun informed himself of his clients' needs before embarking on a design. 'Court or block' will then investigate the thinking behind Lasdun's disposition of the College building on the available site. 'Shaping the College' will pursue this investigation into the location of specific components of the College within that overall shape. The architectural form given to the resulting layout will be analysed in four subsections under the heading 'A building of grace, dignity and charm', and a separate section entitled 'The great art of architecture'. A final section on 'Critical reception' will recount some of the responses the building has enjoyed from its design stage through to the present. After this will come the 'Guide' in which the building will be discussed first from the exterior, and then room by room inside.

Architect and client

Once appointed, Lasdun approached the briefing process not as a tedious but necessary enquiry into the number and type of rooms required, but as the formative inspiration for his design work, and the physicians for their part stuck by their resolution to accept a modernist building, giving Lasdun an enviable freedom to shape the College. This unusual level of trust in their architect may have mirrored their attitude to specialism in the medical world: they were Lasdun's patients, and they put themselves in his hands. Over the years Lasdun was to become friends with many of them, and in 1975 was made an Honorary Fellow of the College in recognition of his contribution to the organisation.

The briefing and design processes through which the building took its form are exceptionally well-recorded in Lasdun's archive at the Royal Institute of British Architects (RIBA) Drawings and Archives Collections. In most architectural papers spoken exchanges disappear from the record, but Lasdun kept lively memoranda of such discussions, giving his opinions at each stage of the design development and preserving a uniquely clear record of the day-to-day business of producing serious architecture. Lasdun's memos, made to enable his office to track the complex process of client consultation which shaped the design, have become a rich source for historians.

By spring 1959 the President was able to inform the College that 'Mr. Lasdun had been taking the greatest care to study the functions, traditions and ceremonies of this old society'.[5] He had indeed, attending dinners and ceremonies, and simply spending time in their current building watching how physicians used it.[6] Lasdun believed in the authority of the good architect, but for him that authority lay in the architect's application of specialist skills, knowledge and artistry to the precise needs and wishes of a building's future users. For Lasdun these included wishes and needs of which the client was unaware, but which the architect's trained eye could observe or intuit. Speaking about the College shortly after its completion, Lasdun told his audience of architects that 'our job is to give the client, on time and on cost, not what he wants but what he never dreamed he wanted and, when he gets it, he recognises it as something he wanted all the time'.[4]

Court or block?

The site made available for the new College profited from the beauty of Nash's Regent's Park, but also threatened the potential constraints of such historic surroundings. In 1957 the Crown Estate Commissioners had decided to preserve and restore the Nash terraces as far as possible, minimising modern additions or replacements.[7] In the 1950s the site chosen for the College was still occupied by Someries House, a Nash building much altered and neglected, bomb-damaged, and declared unworthy of preservation in the 1947 Gorell Report on Regent's Park.[8] Lasdun delighted in quoting John Summerson's account of it as a home for 'superannuated governesses'.[9] Even with it gone, however, there would be a major challenge accommodating the new

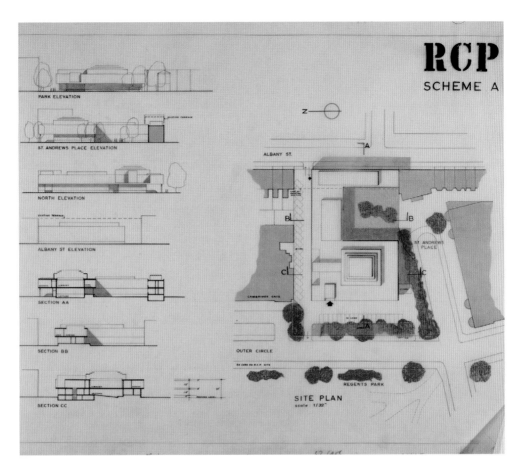

RCP
SCHEME A

PARK ELEVATION

ST. ANDREWS PLACE ELEVATION

NORTH ELEVATION

ALBANY ST ELEVATION

SECTION AA

SECTION BB

SECTION CC

ALBANY ST.

ST ANDREWS PLACE

CAMBRIDGE GATE

OUTER CIRCLE

REGENTS PARK

SITE PLAN
scale 1/32"

Plan of courtyard scheme for the College, c1959. Regent's Park is at the bottom of the drawing, which shows a three-sided courtyard open to St Andrews Place (RIBA Library Drawings Collection)

building to a site overlooking a major park and facing a particularly charming Nash terrace. One strength of Lasdun's candidacy for this job must have been his recent success in getting all the necessary permissions for an assertively modern block of flats facing Green Park, immediately next to the 18th-century Spencer House.[10]

To the other side of the site was (and is) Cambridge Gate, a large and incongruous Italianate Victorian block. To 1950s tastes this was the purest poison, and Lasdun would have felt that his College needed to turn its back on this, and its face to the park and the Nash terrace. For most of the two-year design period he sought to arrange the new building round a courtyard open at the end towards St Andrews Place, with some of the most important functions in the arm of the College which fronted onto the park on one side and the court on the other.

This court became a central theme of the planning of the College, and made its first datable appearance at a meeting held within three weeks of Lasdun's appointment, when he discussed it over dinner with the Building Committee. His reason for

Left **Front of the College viewed from Cambridge Terrace** (Edwin Smith/RIBA Library Photographs Collection)

turning the focus of the building away from the green west was that 'this particular area of the park has no particular landscape value'. More importantly, however, the court was an end in itself, providing 'a closed precinct, around which all elements faced, creating its own personal environment'. This principle, Lasdun records, 'appeared to be unanimously approved'.[7] At the same time, however (apparently in order to investigate comparative costs), Lasdun continued to develop a parallel scheme for the College building as a free-standing block facing the park.

Lasdun seems to have leaned in favour of the court, guided by his personal sense of the nature of collegiate life; at the same time as he was working on the Royal College of Physicians design he was also producing schemes for two Cambridge colleges.[11] He explained in 1965 that 'a court defines in physical terms a scholastic body, inward looking and protected from traffic noise'.[4] Until the summer of 1959 Lasdun appears to have been steering the Building Committee towards the court solution. However, in May, as the design developed, he abruptly discovered that, in some way which is not made clear in his notes, it was not meeting his standards: 'three weeks ago results of court plan in spite of all efforts NOT ACCEPTABLE, in spite of being workable and decent'.[12] From this crisis seems to have emerged the final outline design, and other tantalisingly obscure notes imply that this may have been the moment when the staircase hall came to its mature form. The following notes appear to be a description of the walk up the stairs from the Censors' Room to the Dorchester Library, referred to here by the name of the governing body of the College which was to meet there, the Comitia: 'clockwise movement around Censor, history, comitia. All chattels, portraits, stained glass in a blaze of light'.[12]

To some extent the finished building retains the idea of an external court. As Lasdun put it, 'the low projection of the lecture hall from the main block preserves the character of a small-scale backwater, a private court'.[4] But the feeling of the embraced area is unmistakably that of a private garden rather than a quadrangle in which physicians might meet in passing and talk. However, Lasdun did not simply abandon his wish for a physical expression of an 'inward-looking' protected space for the learned society. Rather he moved it indoors. In the built design the staircase hall took the role of the court: it was a natural meeting point for intended and accidental encounters, a good place to sit and think or talk, and it was undoubtedly protected and tranquil. Just as the court scheme had placed the important rooms of the College round the open-air quadrangle, so the staircase hall is in the middle of the College's most important spaces – the Library, dining room (Osler Room) and Censors' Room with its 17th-century panelling. The lecture theatre (Wolfson Theatre) is placed to one side to prevent the large outside audiences who would attend the new public discussions there from tramping through, disturbing the peace of the staircase hall.

The staircase hall from the upper gallery (John Donat/RIBA Library Photographs Collection)

The College has changed significantly in its role since the building opened in 1964. Designed as a combination of academic facility and members' club, it has now become a much busier meeting place for all manner of outside events. All the major spaces are now routinely hired out as meeting or lecture rooms, often but not exclusively for medical bodies. With this change the concourse is no longer reliably a quiet place for encounters and thought, but new pleasures can be found in watching visitors moving around the building every day in numbers originally seen only at major ceremonial occasions.

The addition of this important and luxurious indoor void at a relatively late stage in the design process may have been related to the generous benefaction of the Wolfson Foundation. With its strong emphasis on medical facilities and organisations, it made a substantial contribution – the biggest of the Foundation's first decade.[13] They felt that 'generally the scheme should not be stinted for the sake of £15,000 or so'.[14] This backing must have contributed significantly to the high quality of workmanship and materials in the College – things which in other buildings often suffer cuts during last-minute budget reductions.

Shaping the College

The Royal College of Physicians has a quality of apparent simplicity and appropriateness which makes it hard to imagine alternative dispositions. This is the skill of the architect: in fact, during its design, elements of the building were moved all over the place. The Censors' Room, always an important feature, was sometimes in the centre of the park façade, sometimes overlooking the dining hall, and sometimes off the Long Room. The stairs suddenly appeared in their current form after many iterations in a conformation like that of the symmetrical double-stair in the previous College building.[15] The lecture theatre moved from being beneath the centre of the College to its peripheral position as built.

Anatomical table showing the nervous system, 17th century, Italy
(Geremy Butler)

Lasdun recalled that he was helped towards an organic, circulatory way of thinking about the organisation of the principal spaces by his discovery of a set of 17th-century anatomical tables in the old College building.[16] These are circulatory and nervous systems removed from the corpses of executed Italian criminals, and varnished onto boards in order to provide medical teaching tools. They are currently displayed on the gallery of the Dorchester Library. These vascular metaphors were particularly apt in an organisation whose most distinguished early member was William Harvey (1578–1657), the first physician to accurately describe the circulation of the blood.

After so much playing around with the spaces, Lasdun achieved in the end a solution of great clarity and elegance. The building is divided into three architecturally distinct zones. The grandest, clad in off-white mosaic tiles, is the ceremonial area, a sort of casket whose ground level floats one and a half storeys above the street, and is the floor level of the dining hall and the Library. These are each double-height spaces, with balconies which run out of them and snake through the staircase hall providing further areas for relaxation and informal talk.

Beneath this white casket is an area clad in dark brick. Here are housed casual common rooms, College offices, the lecture theatre and other such important but quotidian functions. At the rear of the site, facing onto Albany Street, is the third zone – the less grand offices, and (originally) flats for one or two of the College's officers. This block has lower ceiling heights and less luxurious finishes. It acts as a wall insulating the rest of the College from the noisy traffic of Albany Street.

'A building of grace, dignity and charm'

Once Lasdun and his team had worked out an overall disposition for the College's various rooms, the task was to work out what the building would look like. In this, Lasdun faced an unusual challenge for this period of British architecture. Most avant garde architecture of the 1950s, built or not, was designed to be cheap, big, contemporary, of the people, and often with a limited life. A common architectural preoccupation was with repeatability or even a facility to mass produce such buildings. Here, by contrast, Lasdun was asked for a mid-sized, lasting, ceremonious, luxurious home for an elite body which wished to remain in constant touch with its distinguished history: a modernist home for an ancient institution.

Lasdun's challenge was to find an unequivocally modernist language in which not only to display historic objects but to make them genuinely at home, and to devise an appearance for the building which would be proudly contemporary while also achieving a quality of build and aesthetics which would enable it to last a century or more beyond the moment of its creation. The next four sections will look at some of the ways in which he tried to achieve this.

Front of the College showing the overhanging Library and entrance columns (Matthew Weinreb)

Detail of the front showing the expressive power of the entrance columns

The entrance columns

One crucial aspect of the College which needed to set an appropriately high tone was the front to Regent's Park. Lasdun's initial idea for the front of the College was to have the approach and entrance hall overhung by the unsupported volume of the Library. This would have required an exceptional cantilever from the walls at the back of the entrance hall, and the engineers, from the firm Ove Arup & Partners, told him it could not be done.[17] Lasdun started to experiment with adding columns to the front edge of the Library, and drawings survive in his archive showing a pair of columns supporting the lower level, with no support to the upper.[18]

There is another curious piece of evidence of the extent to which Lasdun and his office agonised over the placing and expression of the supports, and dating this stage of the design to December 1959. The implication is that it was sufficiently in the forefront of their minds to have become a shared joke: in Lasdun's papers survives a Christmas card drawn for Lasdun by an anonymous hand, showing the Library supported on a pair of large spheres. The card reads '…99 Cough. Merry Christmas from the Medical Orderlies!'[19]

The eventual solution of three columns rising to the two different heights is one of the most memorable images of the College. Lasdun's initial desire to have the Library floating free would undoubtedly have been spectacular as showpiece engineering, but it would not have had nearly the expressive power of the columns.

The staircase hall from outside. By night the pattern of lighter walls and darker interiors is reversed to delightful effect

A Beaux Arts modernist

When Lasdun was a student at the Architectural Association in the early 1930s the school was still following a curriculum as yet almost untouched by Continental modernism.[20] His formal training was modelled on that developed at the Ecole des Beaux Arts in Paris, an education in classical architecture which made students think about architecture by giving them improbably grand and impractical commissions for buildings like 'An embassy on a rocky promontory'.[21]

Although he left the Architectural Association early in order to work in a practice, Lasdun later acknowledged that this classical training had left an impression on him – especially lessons about the connecting spaces in buildings from the great Edwardian architect, Edwin Landseer Lutyens.[3] This training was one of the resources he drew on when faced with the challenge of the Royal College of Physicians: the emphasis that such curricula placed on ceremonial routes gave Lasdun an underlying principle for organising his building, and equipped him with certain proven techniques for evoking aesthetic responses. Thus the progression from largely symmetrical façade through an enclosed, comparatively dark entrance hall to the light and space of the staircase hall is a typical lesson of the Beaux Arts approach. Another possible example of Beaux Arts influence is the manner in which the main staircase obliges visitors to turn through 270°, scanning the entire hall as they rise.

These classical commonplaces are given new life in Lasdun's interpretation by his eagerness to alter them beyond easy recognition. The influential critic, Reyner Banham (in an article about a Lasdun council estate), called Lasdun's mentor and employer, Berthold Lubetkin, a 'Beaux-Arts modernist', referring to his continuation of some of the aesthetic habits he had learnt during a classical architectural training.[22] In the 1950s and 1960s 'Beaux Arts' was still an insult in modernist mouths – Lasdun would not have wished at this time to be so described. Accordingly, his classical techniques are transformed and obscured: the symmetry of the façade is undercut by the asymmetrical lecture theatre and escape stairs, and the off-centre service tower on the roof; the classical device of framing a door with columns is undermined by blocking the centre with a third column; the entrance door is off axis; and the entrance hall and staircase hall are asymmetrical.

Space and surface

In addition to the pre-modern techniques of his student days, Lasdun also brought into play some characteristic modernist methods to produce the atmosphere he sought. The first of these is the sense of infinitely extending space popularised by Ludwig Mies van der Rohe's 1929 Barcelona Pavilion. There, rather than boxing it in with corners, the architect divided his building with flat partitions implying shafts of uninterrupted space radiating

View from St Andrews Place showing how the Censors' Room appears to 'hover' beneath the upper storey (Royal College of Physicians of London, © John Donat/RIBA Library Photographs Collection)

out into infinity from the pavilion. The floor plan of the partition slabs was reminiscent in plan of the paintings of the Dutch de Stijl movement, an important influence on many modernist architects. The slit views between rooms at the Royal College of Physicians, and out into the city, exhibit this conception of space.

Corners in many parts of the building are cut by slit windows, to reduce the sense of enclosure which a solid corner produces. The flow of space between interior and exterior is assisted by the way in which the glazing of the big windows in the staircase hall does not interrupt the mosaic, implying that the division between inside and out is circumstantial rather than fundamental.

Lasdun acknowledged, too, the influence of Paul Klee's painting on his work.[23] The College has a similar sense of floating blocks of space, for example in the way the Censors' Room appears from outside to hover beneath the volume of the upper storey.

These are techniques that were developed by continental European architects in the 1930s; Lasdun's treatment of surfaces, by contrast, is more characteristically that of the British 1950s avant garde. Many pre-war modernists had finished their buildings in smooth render and white paint, disguising the

Right **View of the corner of the Library from the south side garden** (Royal College of Physicians of London, © John Donat/RIBA Library Photographs Collection)

physical reality of their construction and materials to create an image of abstract white shapes. The post-war generation, who acquired the tag 'Brutalists', took a lead from the 1950s work of their hero the Swiss-French architect Le Corbusier, where the process by which surfaces had been produced was celebrated by leaving them as naked concrete, brick or wood.

Here Lasdun's Baggeridge blue engineering bricks are entirely, almost exaggeratedly brick-like in their rough, hard texture and their solemn colour. Where 1930s architects had used these bricks to create recessed dark plinths and therefore imply a building which floated above the ground, Lasdun celebrates the physicality and weight of the same material. Similarly, his concrete was originally exposed on roof features and fire escape, and bore the marks of the rough wood moulds in which it had been formed. The porcelain mosaic tiles (made in Candolo, near Turin, to a specially commissioned off-white) come closer to the dematerialising white paint of the 1930s, but they nevertheless have a texture, a sheen and a colour.

Where 1930s white-painted cubist buildings had implied a unity of structure, Lasdun makes architectural gestures towards the revelation of structural distinctions. On the exterior of the College, for instance, the rectangular mosaic tiles appear often to cover areas of concrete beam or column, while smaller square tiles clad thin walls. The two are divided by indented shadow gaps. These shallow grooves can be seen throughout the College marking junctions between materials – one of the more striking examples is that dividing the dignified marble stairs down from the entrance hall from the rough blue brick floor beneath. This separation of materials and apparent clarity of structure is characteristic of the 1950s and 1960s when 'honesty' about how a building was put together was regarded as an intrinsically good thing.

A plug-in monument

The near black-and-white of brick and mosaic recalls many of the buildings of Berthold Lubetkin, and Lasdun had himself used these elegant colour contrasts in several projects since leaving Lubetkin's firm. At the Royal College of Physicians, however, the contrasting materials came to represent a manner of thinking about buildings, which Lasdun adapted from Le Corbusier as being particularly appropriate for this job.

In 1931 Le Corbusier had proposed for Algiers an enormous building consisting of a standardised, permanent framework into which temporary structures could be slotted according to the need of the moment.[24] In the late 1950s this idea began to gain increasing currency among younger architects. Here Lasdun takes it to a new level of elegance, as his task requires. The mosaic-clad part of the building floats free of the ground, containing spaces which need never change – dining room, Library and Censors' Room. These house the unchanging functions of the College, and are the seat of its traditions.

Between the legs of this ethereal volume is threaded another architecture, as Lasdun described it, a 'blue brick cradle', 'a do-it-yourself ruin, non-permanent, structurally indeterminate, the brick used for paving as well'.[25] The implication of this distinction was that should the lecture theatre prove too small or be superseded by some unforeseen technology, it could be demolished and replaced with something more appropriate to the conditions of the moment.

The idea is only valid to a certain point within this specific building: the lecture theatre is crucial aesthetically, irrespective of changes in requirements, and it is built to a standard (see pages 31–32) which makes it impossible to imagine casual demolition.

Whether or not Lasdun genuinely contemplated the future destruction of this remarkable piece of craft, however, the notion of a permanent, temple-like core into which could be plugged additional pods at need was clearly a useful inspiration and a visually stimulating organising principle. It has also held good in other parts of the building. In the 1990s Lasdun was called back to add an additional lecture theatre (the Seligman Theatre), an exhibition space for the College's fine silver and the Symons Collection of medical instruments, and most significantly the

The curves of the lecture theatre walls (above) were achieved by the 37 specially designed bricks, some of which are shown in drawing below from the architect's office (Above: The Edge, Cheltenham; below: RIBA Library Drawings Collection)

TYPE	DESCRIPTION	LOCATION	NOTES	TYPE	DESCRIPTION	LOCATION
10	1½" Radius / Bullnosed Stretcher on Flat	Albany Street Block: Internal Window Cill; Kitchen Yard; Staircase 7; Oil Fuel Storage	Standard Smooth Blue Pressed Facing Bricks	17	4¼" / 20° Squint	Lecture Theatre External Window & Entrance Foyer
11	1½" Radius / Bullnose Header on Flat	Ditto	Ditto.	18	4¼" / 11½° Squint	Lecture Theatre External Window & Entrance Foyer
12	½" Radius / Internal Return on Flat	Ditto	Ditto Handed as required	19	4¼" / 70° Squint	Lecture Theatre Internal Window & Entrance Foyer
13	1½" Radius	Ditto	Ditto Handed as Required	20	4¼"	Main Block External Window at Porter

Dining room (Osler Room)
(Royal College of Physicians of London, © John Donat/RIBA Library Photographs Collection)

Council Chamber. At this time Lasdun talked of this extension as the completing element of the design, counterbalancing the Censors' Room.[26] Although there is no direct evidence of a specific intention in the 1950s to add an extension in this location, the point stands that the addition vindicates Lasdun's original idea that the College building would be extendable, and the blue brick areas changeable.

From this rich mix of ideas certain dominant effects emerge. Within the building the most memorable things are the room spaces: the calm dignity of the Library and dining hall, the clarity and promise of the entrance hall, the shock of the Censors' Room, and above all the beautiful void of the staircase hall with its delicate balance of dignity and informality. The experience of moving through these areas is the supreme pleasure of the interior.

Outside, the most memorable thing is perhaps the shape of the main vessel – the apparent simplicity with which Lasdun folds such interesting and successful internal rooms into the consistent profile of the white-tiled casket.

'The great art of architecture'

The Royal College of Physicians came at the end of a decade of experimentation and exploration for Lasdun, during which some of his many designs were much less satisfactory than his later work.[27] Early drawings for the College include some unfortunate similarities to these less successful projects, notably over-done decorative roof structures to mark the important rooms. As he worked on the College design, however, he pared away unnecessary ornament and reduced the scheme to a greater clarity and simplicity.

Despite this, there remains an element of self-conscious art to this building. The materials have a surrealist quality, with brick – a standardised material for building straight walls – eerily distorted while the concrete, which can adopt any shape, is rectilinear. Marble appears to have been bent in the handrails on the stairs, or to form a sliding partition (permanently open) in front of the Censors' Room. To achieve these effects Lasdun fights his materials: the complex curve of the brick is produced only at the cost of remarkable labour from architects, brick-makers and brick-layers. Some of these aesthetic decisions barely nod to function; although Lasdun pointed to the internal corridor and robing room as justifications for the asymmetric plan of the lecture room, it does not explain the twisting of the external walls.

In his later work smaller budgets and bigger projects obliged him to abandon such magnificent craft techniques, leaving the College uniquely artistic in Lasdun's work. It is hard to say whether, had there been further such commissions, he would have continued along this craft path, or whether he would have restrained himself in response to the mild criticisms which these features received from some architects at the time. Lasdun looked back at the College in 1965, saying that 'before I forget the bloody struggles of its design, I shall have to return and feed back to myself the devastating lesson that all of us have to accept – that the great art of architecture is the art of concealing the art of architecture'.[4]

The integration of structure, services, building process and function into a magnificent overall shape is more completely achieved in his later buildings for the University of East Anglia and the National Theatre in London than at the Royal College of Physicians. However, this later work generally offers less of the joy of beautiful craft to the viewer, and is perhaps less accessible with its rougher materials, cheaper fittings and, in most cases, necessarily modest internal spaces. It was here at the Royal College of Physicians that he was given the most freedom, and so here that he could discover to the full his own architectural personality. The College shows all of the love of paradox, the excitement of contrasting spaces, the juxtaposition of harsh and welcoming façades, the shaping of external spaces, and the mastery of composition, which were to characterise his work for the following two decades.

Right **View from the fire escape stairs towards Regent's Park** (Royal College of Physicians of London, © John Donat/RIBA Library Photographs Collection)

Critical reception

What did the physicians think of Lasdun's schemes? Several of them, notably the Treasurer, Richard Bomford, were strongly supportive from the start. Others initially appeared fractionally less sure, but gave it their full backing – the President, moderniser though he was, sounded as if he was reassuring himself as much as the architect when he wrote to Lasdun in May 1960 telling him 'it grows on me. I am sure it is a masterpiece'.[28] The response of one Building Committee member indicates the extent both of Lasdun's success in explaining his scheme, and of the entrenched opposition he faced: one of Lasdun's pithily amusing memoranda records that this Fellow 'thought the building fitted its context admirably, was generally splendid, sculpturally beautiful, but dislikes modern architecture'.[29]

The building work began on schedule in September 1961, but, as was universal with building projects of the period, finished late, in 1964.[30] After a Royal opening on 5 November 1964, the physicians themselves moved into their new home.[31] Any remaining doubters seem rapidly to have been swayed by the beauty of their surroundings, and the College has been happy with and proud of its home ever since. By the 1980s water had, in places, reached the reinforcing steel in the concrete, rusting it and breaking off bits of concrete and the areas of tile which cover them; the College simply repaired the concrete and procured exact replacements for the missing tiles. The repairs are only detectable from their slightly newer appearance.

The building received large amounts of attention from the outside world. In a few cases responses were hostile: an article entitled 'Sausage factory – or architecture of international standing?' quoted an anonymous member of the public complaining of the back of the College to Albany Street that 'this was an elegant, gracious street and now they slap us in the face with this thing. In place of our beautiful houses they have thrown up an almost solid wall with high, tiny windows like a prison.'[32] By and large, though, the building enjoyed warm admiration receiving, along with the praise of commentators and journalists, a 1964 RIBA London Architecture medal, and a Civic Trust Award for 1967. The College was discussed in architectural magazines all round the world, and raised Lasdun's international reputation to the point where in 1966 an autograph hunter in India successfully got a note to Lasdun with the address reading only 'Denys Lasdun, Well-known British architect'.[33]

Nor was the success of the building short-lived: it has moved from the status of exciting newcomer to classic, gaining the RIBA Trustees Medal (an award given to buildings in recognition of their success and quality over time) in 1992, and becoming one of the first post-war buildings to be given statutory protection at Grade I in 1998.

The opinions of others are not the final test, though. As Lasdun himself said, 'You can go and see it, and the building, if it has anything to say, will have to speak for itself'.[34]

Guide to the building

The Regent's Park front

The most memorable image of the Royal College of Physicians is its front towards Regent's Park, generally seen from an oblique angle because of mature trees. The various oppositions in the College's architecture are clear from here. There is the contrast between blue brick and white mosaic; between brick which should be straight but curves, and tiled concrete which could be curved but is straight. There is the contrast between the floating volume of the Library on its slender columns and the sombre heavy mound of the lecture theatre block on the right of the main building (in the picture opposite and on pages 34–35), which appears to have distorted and sunk into the car park under its own dark weight.

This is not easy or pretty architecture but architecture which seeks to engage the senses, mind and emotion of the viewer. The Library front, elegant and symmetrical in its white classicism, is at the same time stretched and anxious. The columns on which it stands seem too thin to support it, and one of them disconcerts by breaking the rule of classical architecture that an entrance must be flanked in the middle by paired columns, not obstructed by one. The way in which columns meet beams flush and without a separating line produces a curious feeling that the front is paper-thin, not solid. The blind face above the columns has a larger gap than expected between its unrevealing slit windows, which combines with the over-long columns to give a feeling of brittle attenuation. Above this fragile-looking composition stands a palpably solid concrete service tower with a pair of semi-cylinders at its western end. The protective coating on this has reduced the clarity of its shuttering marks and diminished the contrast between it and the mosaic, but the intended effect can still be imagined. This weighty and oversized element sitting off-centre adds to the feeling of fragility in the façade, and undercuts its formal symmetry. Beneath the façade the dark materials of the entrance are almost lost in shade. It is an intriguing composition, and makes the viewer want to know more.

This kind of strong composition in which recognisable elements are made surprising and emotionally charged by subtle changes and unexpected juxtaposition recalls the work of the English Baroque architect Nicholas Hawksmoor, whom Lasdun greatly admired.[35] In the floating strata there may be a hint of borrowings from Frank Lloyd Wright's houses around Chicago, which Lasdun had visited on his honeymoon in 1954.

The north front

This side of the building faces parking and a service yard. The fire stairs were originally in exposed concrete – 'the only material likely to weather with time'.[4] This would have developed a contrast to the perfect, unchanging mosaic, but the concrete is now covered in a creamy protective paint.

Behind the stairs is the Council Chamber, Lasdun's last addition to the College before his death in 2001. The extension represents a

Front north-west corner view from the Park, showing the double-storey Library (Matthew Weinreb)

partial vindication of Lasdun's belief that the blue brick areas offered potential for future expansion and growth (see pages 24–25). A close look at the brickwork which supports the Chamber reveals the difference in date between extension and original College: the new bricks are slightly smaller – the metric brick size adopted in 1974, rather than the older imperial brick.

The south front

This side of the building rewards considerable inspection. Firstly, there is the magnificent brickwork of the lecture theatre (see pages 34–35). These are Baggeridge blue engineering bricks, with their distinctive hard, slightly glossy texture and resistance to weathering or wear. The pointing is recessed from the brick surface, producing a strongly textured effect like rusticated stone on a classical building. Especially in contrast to the orderly perfection of the mosaic-covered building above, the lecture theatre seems graceless, heavy and contorted; the walls do not merely lean in, they twist through their length in a manner that is structurally disconcerting (it is achieved by laying them as a facing on a supporting concrete wall).

The brick is worked to a remarkably high standard: 37 different types of brick were specially designed by the architects and baked by the manufacturers to achieve the curves and corners of the brickwork without having to cut bricks (a cut surface has a markedly

View of south side garden looking towards the Nash terraces (Royal College of Physicians of London, © John Donat/RIBA Library Photographs Collection)

different texture from a baked one). In addition, the perfectionism of the site architects was such that many bricks were rejected for being visually sub-standard. Edward Cullinan, a young architect in Lasdun's office at the time, carried away (by repeated journeys in his Morris 1000 van) the numerous rejects to pave the surroundings and ground floor of his own house in Camden, with some left over for his smallholding on the North Staffordshire Moors.[36]

Further up St Andrews Place you reach the garden, recently planted with herbs and flowers with strong medical associations. The College, substantially closed to the west, is very open here, with enormous windows looking out over the greenery at several levels. Penetrating the largest glazed area is the Censors' Room. Seen by Lasdun as the inner sanctum of the building, its structure is visually separated from that of the rest of the College to emphasise this special quality. In the evening the lit staircase hall which surrounds it becomes more visible from the street outside, to beautiful effect.

Lasdun had seen St Andrews Place as an architectural entity, although at the time the Nash houses were not associated with the College. In subsequent decades the College acquired them, leading to the formal recognition in 1984 of this as a 'medical precinct' and the removal of the dividing wall (see above image).

To the east of the Censors' Room the primary structural system of the building is exposed: mosaic-covered concrete columns at intervals of about 23 feet, with the uppermost storey overhanging.

The back

After the mixed white and dark blue of the other elevations, the back of the building to Albany Street is a shock. It has no mosaic, and none of the lightness of the St Andrews Place side. At the end of a terrace in light stucco the College office building's dark, closed face is an act of violence against its neighbours – the more so since ten of the original Georgian terraced houses were pulled down to create it. Where the terrace has a gentle rhythm of repeated vertical windows, Lasdun's block has uninterrupted strip windows, and a single small entrance. At street level there is only wall, no window, and the vehicle entrance to the service yard is just a blank hole, lacking any framing.

The Albany Street elevation caused controversy at the design stage among the Royal Fine Art Commission, a distinguished aesthetic judging panel one of whose members at the time was Basil Spence, architect of Coventry Cathedral. Lasdun defended the design, but 'Spence was still "unhappy" about it. I said I could do nothing about his "unhappiness" and left it at that. I did not wish to change the elevation'.[37]

Why was Lasdun determined to treat Albany Street with apparent hostility? The answer probably lies in his thinking about the nature of college communities: 'a court defines in physical terms a scholastic body, inward looking and protected from traffic noise'.[4] 'Inward looking and protected' has a marked implication of defensiveness. If the collegiate space is to be cocooned, bright and quiet, Lasdun felt the need for some kind of defensive wall to keep it that way. The blind wall of the lecture theatre and the few windows of the Library protect the College from the quieter road next to Regent's Park, but the more solid and forbidding insulation of these alarming office blocks, both at a simple acoustic level and at an aesthetic and symbolic one, is required to exclude the noisy corridor-street behind. There is an equivocal indication in an article reporting a Lasdun talk that he may have referred to it as the College's 'get lost elevation'.[25]

The College from Albany Street
(Royal College of Physicians of London, © John Donat/RIBA Library Photographs Collection)

Overleaf **Front of the College from Park Square East showing the brickwork of the lecture theatre**
(Bernard Cox/RIBA Library Photographs Collection)

Entrance hall

Entering the building from Regent's Park, the visitor passes through glass doors between walls of blue brick. The walls, however, do not reach the ceiling, leaving instead a strip of glass at the top to indicate that they perform no structural role in supporting the great span above.

As visitors pass from the open sky of the street beneath the overhanging Library and up a few steps to the entrance hall, they become progressively more enclosed. The few steps up to the concourse level (shown opposite) bring the ceiling still closer, then all is revealed in the triple-height space of the staircase hall, with vast windows bringing in the outside world, and the galleries above stepping out to enlarge the space further. The brick walls and sturdy metal-work continue the vocabulary of external landscaping to the entrance area, but the floor of the entrance hall is paved in marble, introducing the more sumptuous feel of the staircase hall above.

The original reception desk in the entrance hall

The detailing of the entrance hall, as with all the detailing in the College, is impressive, with the brick screen behind the reception desk pierced by two vertical slits like a castle's arrow-loops, a recurrent motif in Lasdun's work. The original desk (replaced to accommodate increasing demands) was an elegantly minimal stone table reminiscent of an altar (shown left). Another recent alteration can be seen in the lifts introduced in the entrance hall and next to the outside entrance steps to provide access for all via the same route.

As you mount the stairs, the attractive bright colours of Keith New's stained glass window burst upon you from the right, a premonition of smaller panels of old glass in the staircase hall, salvaged from former homes of the College.

Looking from the entrance hall up the steps to the staircase hall, a slit view gives a clear line of sight right through to the first floor dining hall. This view is beautifully composed, and was exploited by the great post-war architectural photographer Henk Snoek. Notice in the photograph opposite that the ceiling was originally tiled in rough-textured cork, now replaced with plaster. Where smooth white plaster asks only not to be noticed, the original cork gave a texture and reality to the ceiling characteristic of the expressive use of materials favoured by Lasdun and other architects of the 1950s and 1960s.

Stained glass in the entrance hall by Keith New

Wolfson Theatre

While the number and scale of outside conferences and events held at the College has increased enormously since the 1960s, the original layout nevertheless made provision for non-Fellows to attend lectures and discussions there. This was an architectural expression of the modernising President's desire to increase the College's engagement with wider debates on public health. For this purpose the Wolfson Theatre (the main lecture theatre) is approached without passing through the inner collegiate spaces,

View from the entrance hall into the staircase hall (Henk Snoek/RIBA Library Photographs Collection)

allowing large external groups to come to lectures without disturbing the peace of the rest of the College.

The route from entrance hall to lecture theatre divides round a spiral staircase down to the cloakroom level. This stair is of the most luxurious finish, with the white marble of its inner handrail curving sensuously with the descent. The perfection of marble and white tile is heightened by contrast with the blue brick of the floor below.

The lecture theatre itself was built to a high acoustic and technological standard and, as ever, attractively detailed. Both wood and glass curve elegantly round the corner of the projection room, for instance.

Left **The spiral staircase down from the Wolfson Theatre lobby, a contrast of rough, dark brick and bright tile and marble** (Royal College of Physicians of London, © John Donat/RIBA Library Photographs Collection)

Right **Wolfson Theatre**

The pale blonde hardwood of the theatre and its furnishings is Tasmanian oak (in fact a type of eucalyptus) donated by the Royal Australian College of Physicians. The President's substantial throne, which is stored in the corridor outside the theatre, is Lasdun's only executed chair design.

Censors' Room

The Censors' Room, with its antique furniture and 17th-century panelling brought from the earlier homes of the College

This room comes as a surprise: after the high, bright space of the staircase hall it is lower and dark; after the light, modern tile it is wainscoted in dark wood. The Spanish oak panelling has travelled with the College from home to home since the 1670s building by Robert Hooke, but surely it has never been as surprising as it is at the heart of Lasdun's building. He allows it to retain its dignity

Busts of Richard Mead (foreground) and Matthew Baillie in the Censors' Room

while unmistakably placing it in quotation marks by punching through it a few of his distinctive slit windows. Lasdun's mention of a need to 'unite hostile elements' may refer to the challenge of introducing such a foreign component into his design.[38] If so, he certainly brought it to a good resolution, producing a startling contrast on entering or leaving the Censors' Room.

The original purpose of the Censors' Room was for the final *viva voce* examination of those seeking to join the Membership. This exam was legendary in its difficulty and importance, and if you failed you could never reach the top in your field.[39] If you passed, on the other hand, you were admitted to the prestigious body and its luxurious premises. Lasdun himself felt that he had some insight into this experience, as it was in the Trafalgar Square incarnation of the Censors' Room that he had been interviewed for the job of architect for the new building.

Early proposals for the room omitted the ante-chambers, but a humanitarian on the Building Committee objected: 'the point being that if after examination the decision is "fail", the person concerned must be told in privacy, not on the Foyer of the College'.[40]

The ceremony then involved going to the Library. In the previous College this was a simple shuffle next door, but Lasdun decided to dramatise this moment of life-changing ascension with the staircase hall.

Marble Hall

The staircase hall, known today as the Marble or the Marble Hall, is both physically and aesthetically the central space of the College. Lasdun recalled after the building was completed that it had originally grown out of a mention of 'provision for the usual staircases etc'.[4] While the phrase does not appear in surviving versions of the written briefing document, the account tells a remarkable truth: Lasdun added this space on his own initiative, and the physicians supported him. It takes a superior quality of client and a good budget to accept so substantial an addition to the programme, and it was their courage in backing Lasdun that enabled him to give them such a fine building.

The staircase hall is the main component in Lasdun's attempt to solve the central problem of this job: in an age when architecture sought to deflate pretension and throw out tradition, Lasdun was asked to provide a dignified setting for gowned processions and a home for the physical reminders of a long history. Lasdun may well have felt some strain from the challenge of producing a modern building for such a client.

At the simplest level, the staircase hall provides a dignified setting through the use of attractively-grained white Sicilian marble for the floors and the wall outside the Censors' Room. The intrinsic beauty of marble, its cost and its associations with expensive

The three-storey void of the staircase hall showing balconies on each level (Barratts Photo Press Ltd)

formality going back to Greece and Rome instantly proclaim this to be an important place. The gold-coloured handrails on the stairs are presumably intended to add to this sense of luxury. It is not these features, however, which give the hall its quality. There is indeed almost something too luxurious about them – a kind of excessive slickness in their conventional expression of expenditure, foreign to Lasdun's normal tough surfaces and hard expression.

The real dignity of the hall comes from its use of space. This can be a slippery architectural term, but in this case it is literal – the hall uses a lot of space. The shaping of the three-storey void, with balconies stepping further out at each level, contributes to a feeling of generous and relaxed dignity rare in the generally economical buildings of the period.

The quantity of space gives to the pictures and busts in the hall something of the spirit of their earlier surroundings in big rooms; large portraits need space, and large, elegant spaces profit from big portraits. Lasdun said of the staircase hall that 'this kind of space needs people'.[4] When the hall is populated with current physicians, and its walls with the distinguished dead, there is a sense of an ongoing community of physicians through the centuries.

The staircase itself embodies Lasdun's original inspiration that the organising principle of the building should be the process of examination and initiation, leading from Censors' Room to Library. Thus the stairs face the door of the Censors' Room, and spiral through just under one revolution to face the door of the Library. As the members of the processions walk up the stairs the portraits are passed before their eyes. No part of the staircase is overhung by anything, revealing the full height of the space at all times.

Overleaf **Marble staircase, view from the Council Chamber**

The outer balustrade of the staircase is squared-off. The inner balustrade, however, is curved, perhaps in a reminder of the Continental Baroque staircases which Lasdun's architectural mentor, Berthold Lubetkin, so admired. The marble capping is very elegantly worked on these curves, but there is perhaps slightly too much feeling of self-conscious 'art' in this detail: in his later work Lasdun cut out such indulgences.

This central social space profits from enormous windows overlooking the garden and the Nash terraces opposite – windows so big that today's glass producers would find them hard to manufacture. These admit so much natural light that the floor of the hall feels almost like an outdoor space, an illusion enhanced by the detailing: where a traditional building might have had brick outside and plaster in, Lasdun carries his mosaic straight past the glass into the interior walls, minimising the division between interior and exterior, and suggesting visually that the windows are only a climatic necessity, not an architectural division.

View from St Andrews Place
(Royal College of Physicians of London, © John Donat/RIBA Library Photographs)

Dorchester Library

Above **The Dorchester Library gallery**

Below **The Dorchester Library with the portrait of Harvey in the lower left-hand corner**

As one approaches the Dorchester Library, the stairs to the upper gallery of the staircase hall and Library are to the left. These run in two flights up an austere tiled box, but they are given drama and beauty by the lighting, which comes from a concealed skylight flush with the end wall. As twilight falls the skylight is supplemented in the same place by down-lighters to retain the effect. This sort of mysterious lighting may derive from European Baroque church architecture, the best-known example being Bernini's St Theresa, or it may have reached Lasdun via the dramatic side chapels at Le Corbusier's 1950s pilgrimage church at Ronchamp.

The Library itself is entered through double doors which, like most of the wood in the College, are of rich brown East African muninga. The doors pivot elegantly a few inches from the wall, and in tall glass panels at each hinge pick up the theme of viewing slits common in Lasdun's architecture at the College and elsewhere.

One of the most institutionally important spaces of the College, the Library is also one of the most architecturally conservative. The walls are lined with the magnificent books given by the Marquis of Dorchester to replace the collection donated by William Harvey but destroyed in the Great Fire of London. Photographs of the College's previous Library in Pall Mall East reveal affinities between the two, each rectangular, double-height rooms with a gallery giving access to the higher books.[15] Each is entered at the middle of one long side, and opposite hangs a portrait of Harvey saved by the College Librarian from the 1666 fire.[41]

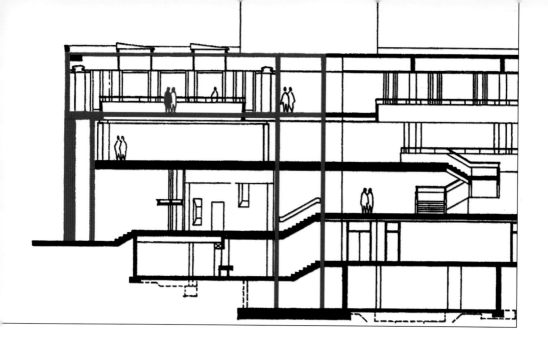

In this cut-through of the Library
seen from the St Andrews Place
side, the parts coloured in red are
carrying the weight of the red-
coloured people down to the
ground from the Library balcony
where they stand. Some of the
weight is carried over to the
supporting walls on the right,
but the rest has to go round the
corner to the blue columns in the
centre of the Regent's Park front

This sort of visual echo recalls advice that Lasdun was given by the excellent Dr Bomford, Treasurer during the design process, that 'as far as possible, all visual/historical/artistic articles should find a place somewhere throughout the building' as this would 'help facilitate the transition in Members' minds from the old to the new building'.[42] The immediate sense of familiarity which even the most conservative Fellows would have felt in entering the new Library was intended, as it were, to butter their paws and make them feel at home.

One difference from the older Library is that where the earlier room was rectangular with the balcony projecting into the room, Lasdun's upper walls step back, avoiding a dark overhang. This seems a simple matter, and the room feels like a solidly built traditional space, perhaps of stone or brick. However, comparison of the exterior of the building with the internal space shows that the engineering of this room is virtuosically complex. In fact, the Library stands at the Regent's Park end on beams, which balance on the slim central columns by the entrance to the building. At the other end the floor beams land on a wall. This makes for an unsupported span of 43 feet for the floor, and 49 feet for the galleries and roof. To support this balcony and others in the building, the walls of the top storey are filled with pre-tensioned steel reinforcement – the walls and some of the weight of the uppermost balconies hang from the roof above rather than standing on the column below.[43] In other words, as you stand on the gallery of the Library your weight (and that of the books and the building itself) is being carried along to the end, round the corner (which is weakened by slit windows), and along to the centre. The apparent simplicity of the space was achieved by

Denys Lasdun's Royal College of Physicians

The Library roof during construction, showing the 49-foot concrete beams which were made elsewhere and lifted into place by crane (Royal College of Physicians)

massive engineering feats involving reinforced concrete beams nearly 50 feet long being lowered into place by cranes.

The slit windows which, seen from outside, form part of an irregular pattern along the top floor now turn out to have a concealed order: they are symmetrically arranged within the Library itself: the classical formality of the Library is preserved, but the exterior has the apparently haphazard window-openings of Le Corbusier's post-war Maisons Jaoul.

Partly to conserve the books and partly, as one commentator speculated, in order that the important meetings there should not suffer the distraction of a view, these windows are few and small.[44] From those which look towards Regent's Park you can judge whether Lasdun was right to turn the communal spaces away from the park. His feeling was that even when the trees were without leaves, 'once you've seen the view for a few minutes it is boring, there are a few trees there, there's nothing magical'.[45]

From the windows to the south can be seen the roof of the Wolfson Theatre. Structurally, this roof is a 'space frame' – a type of steel scaffold popular in the 1950s and 1960s – but it is concealed above and below by solid facings. Lasdun had originally hoped to clad it externally in copper, which would have introduced a surprising green to the colour palette of the building. Its octagonal form may be a subtle reference to the anatomy theatre of Robert Hooke's 1670s College building.[16]

On the Library's upper gallery are displayed the Italian anatomical tables, which Lasdun claimed as an influence in his thinking of the College building as an organism (see page 17).

The front wall of the Library under construction. The curving tubes are the sheaths of steel reinforcing rods carrying the weight of the wall and floors to the columns in the middle. Concrete was then poured around this metal framework to form the wall. The reinforcing rods were then pulled very tight to hold the wall together under the great strain of the wide cantilever (Royal College of Physicians)

Overleaf **Osler Room banquet**

The Osler Room, showing the alignment of roof lights and vertical strip glazing above the door, which together imply a vertical slice of space cutting through the building. The hydraulic wall is shown raised above the two pillars on the left, uniting the dining area with the **Long Room** (Royal College of Physicians of London, © John Donat/RIBA Library Photographs Collection)

Osler and Long Rooms

The Osler Room and Long Room are generally two separate rooms, the latter for pre-dinner drinks, the former for dinner itself. However, for very large dinners, exam sittings and other functions requiring a big space, the wall which divides them can be raised hydraulically to provide a room the width of the building.

The Long Room provides pleasant views over the Nash terrace opposite. It is a good place from which to appreciate Lasdun's attempt to match the materials of his building with those of its surroundings: not only did his tiles echo the colour of the stucco (until the Crown Estates changed their paint colour for the present slightly pinkish cream) but his blue brick picks up the slate of the roofs visible above the plastered façades, and his humped lecture theatre recalls their hipped profile.

In the Osler Room the carpet is a replica of the original. Although this is not covered by the statutory protection afforded the building, the College rightly feels that these fabrics are important elements of Lasdun's vision for the interiors. The staircase hall carpet, originally ginger, may with repeated replacements have shifted to a more golden colour.

In this generous, double-height dining space the balconies combine with a full-height slit window to the staircase hall to make people into theatre for each other. Lasdun observed that 'they have large receptions when the whole building is used: people are in the galleries, on the floor, and there is a communion between people across rooms and into the next room'.[46] This is the practical effect of Lasdun's characteristically modernist composition of extended shafts of space pushing out in all directions. Notice above, for example, the alignment of the roof-lights on the horizontal plane with the slit window above the door in the vertical, implying a continuous vertical slit running long-ways through the building and out.

Council Chamber

This was Lasdun's last addition to the College, and one of his last buildings, added in 1998 to provide an appropriately meditative and distinguished setting for meetings of the College Council. Lasdun spoke of the Council Chamber counterbalancing the Censors' Room across the staircase hall.[47]

In his later years one of Lasdun's principal architectural wishes was to build a religious space of some sort.[48] His wonderful 1980 scheme for a synagogue in Jerusalem fell through for reasons of political instability, and he never did build any kind of church or temple. In this room he aimed for something of the tranquil and ethereal feeling of a sacred space – his own favoured comparison was with a monastic or cathedral chapter house. There is also something rather sci-fi about the feeling of this room with its lighting, ring of tables, and technological-looking Eames chairs.

Council Chamber showing clerestory which produces diffused daylight round the walls of the Chamber
(The Edge, Cheltenham)

Left **Council Chamber dome at night** (Niall Clutton)

Marked out from the rest of the College by its circular plan, the Council Chamber is something of a surprise after its comparatively modest doors. Light falls from a concealed clerestory onto the walls, which are panelled in grey with occasional interruptions for windows like loopholes. The main ceiling is a low dome supported on round-shouldered pointed concrete arches – perhaps a reference to Gothic vaulting ribs.

Only a few years after completing this addition, Lasdun died. His memorial was held at the College and, as a last tribute to a man who had done so much to shape the recent and future history of their institution, the furniture in the staircase hall was removed; Lasdun had long felt that the College used too much of it and that it detracted from the open feeling of his spaces.[49]

Lasdun's relationship with the Royal College of Physicians was exceptionally close and long-lasting. As the extension was being built, Lasdun gave a talk in which he looked back over the course of his long association with the physicians: 'I am deeply grateful to the College for its monumental act of faith when, in 1958, it commissioned me to design such a modern building, and for offering me the opportunity to complete the building as I had originally envisaged it'.[50]

Council Chamber, axial view (Niall Clutton)

References

1 Letter from DN Cole to Lasdun, 1 February 1985, RIBA LaD/28/1.

2 Letter from Lasdun to Platt, 25 August 1958; Lasdun enclosed a copy of *Architectural Design* February 1958, which published a number of Lasdun projects, RIBA LaD/16/5; letter from Dr RR Bomford, Treasurer, to Lasdun, 17 October 1958, RIBA LaD/16/5.

3 Lever J. *National life story collection: architect's lives: Sir Denys Lasdun: interviewed by Jill Lever* (copies in British Library and RIBA LaD/238/6), p 68.

4 Lasdun D. His approach to architecture. *Architectural Design* June 1965;35:272.

5 Lasdun's copy of College Meeting minutes, May 28 1959, RIBA LaD/16/5.

6 For example, Lasdun memorandum, 7 November 1958, recording a dinner on 5 November with Building Committee and President, RIBA LaD/16/5.

7 Saunders A. *Regent's Park: a study of the development of the area from 1086 to the present day*. London, Newton Abbot: David and Charles, 1969:169.

8 Saunders A (ed). *The London County Council Bomb Damage Map, 1935–1945*. London: London Topographical Society, 2005.

9 Lasdun, notes for a lecture to the Architectural Association, 20 February 1964, notes 12 December 1963, RIBA LaD/25/5; the term is first recorded in Lasdun's notes of a lecture by Summerson on 13 November 1962, notes from 14 November, RIBA LaD/25/5.

10 Letter from Lasdun to Platt enclosing details of Lasdun buildings with the Green Park flats highlighted, 4 September 1958, RIBA LaD/16/5.

11 Calder B. 'A terrible battle with architecture': Denys Lasdun in the 1950s, 2. *Architectural Research Quarterly*, in press.

12 Lasdun notes for a committee meeting, 11 June 1959, RIBA LaD/17/4.

13 *The Wolfson Foundation* 1955–2005: *a historical perspective*. London: Wolfson Foundation, 2005:8.

14 Meeting with representatives of the Wolfson Trust and RCP, 22 July 1959, Lasdun memorandum same day, RIBA LaD/17/1, p 1.

15 Offprint of an article by Gordon Nares on the Trafalgar Square College from *Country Life*, 27 March 1953, RIBA LaD/29/2.

16 Lasdun D. Completing the College. *Journal of the Royal College of Physicians of London* 1996;30:293.

17 Michael Bussell, who worked for Ove Arup & Partners from later in the 1960s, recalled hearing this from those involved (personal communication, 31 August 2007).

18 RIBA PB892/2(1).

19 RIBA LaD/17/1.

20 Calder B. The education of an architect: Denys Lasdun in the 1930s. *Twentieth Century Society Journal* 2007;8:117–27.

21 Richards JM. *Memoirs of an unjust fella*. London: Weidenfeld and Nicolson, 1980:43.

22 Banham R. Façade: elevational treatment of the Hallfield Estate Paddington. *Architectural Review* 1954;116:305.

23 Curtis W. *Denys Lasdun: architecture, city, landscape*. London: Phaidon, 1994:67.

24 Banham R. *Megastructure: urban futures of the recent past*. London: Thames and Hudson, 1976:8–9.

25 Sturgess T. Lasdun on the Royal College of Physicians. *Architect's Journal* 29 July 1964:255.

26 Lasdun D. Completing the College. *Journal of the Royal College of Physicians of London* 1996;30:294.

27 Calder B. 'Unlearning lessons': Denys Lasdun in the 1950s, part 1, *Architectural Research Quarterly* 2007; 3/4:301-10: Calder B. 'A terrible battle with architecture': Denys Lasdun in the 1950s, part 2, *Architectural Research Quarterly*, in press.

28 Letter from Platt to Lasdun, 14 May 1960, LaD/17/1.

29 Building Committee meeting 12 May 1960, Lasdun memorandum 16 May, LaD/17/1.

30 Lasdun memorandum 7 November 1958 recording a dinner 5 November with Building Committee and President, RIBA LaD/16/5 p. 5; letter from JL Cook to Peter Softley, 21 September 1961, RIBA LaD/17/2.

31 Letter from Bomford to Lasdun, 10 July 1964, RIBA LaD/25/6.

32 Weston T. Sausage factory – or architecture of international standing. *Medical News* 25 September 1964;12:25.

33 RIBA LaD/26/6.

34 Lasdun D. His approach to architecture. *Architectural Design* June 1965;35;271.

35 Lasdun wrote of his influences in a letter to DN Cole, Harveian Librarian of the Royal College of Physicians, 14 November 1984, RIBA LaD/27/6.

36 Letter from Edward Cullinan to Barnabas Calder, September 2007.

37 Meeting with the RFAC, 9 March 1960, Lasdun memorandum 10 March, RIBA LaD/18/2.

38 Lasdun, notes for a lecture to the Architectural Association, 20 February 1964, notes 12 December 1963, RIBA LaD/25/5.

39 Maxwell R. Royal College of Physicians, Regent's Park, London. *Architectural Review* April 1965;137:269–70.

40 Denys Lasdun memorandum, 12 June 1959, of Building Committee meeting on 11 June, RIBA LaD/16/5.

41 Wolstenholme G. *The Royal College of Physicians of London portraits.* London: J & A Churchill, 1964:204.

42 Meeting between Bomford and Lasdun, 29 March 1960, Lasdun memorandum 30 March, RIBA LaD/17/1.

43 Lasdun memorandum of a telephone conversation with 'Ross' of Arup, 22 January 1960, RIBA LaD/25/5.

44 Maxwell R. Royal College of Physicians, Regent's Park, London. *Architectural Review* April 1965;137:270.

45 Denys Lasdun interviewed by an editor for 'Royal College'. *Architect and Building News* 29 June 1960:826.

46 Denys Lasdun interviewed by an editor for 'Royal College'. Architect and Building News 29 June 1960:827.

47 Lasdun D. Completing the College. *Journal of the Royal College of Physicians of London* 1996;30:294.

48 Lever interview, op cit, 102.

49 Interview with Glen Price, Building Services Manager of the College, Summer 2004.

50 Denys Lasdun. Completing the College. *Journal of the Royal College of Physicians of London* 1996;30:295.

College homes, 1518–1964

The Stone House, Knightrider Street

The Royal College of Physicians occupied four homes in London before its move to Regent's Park in 1964. The College's first premises were provided by its founder, Thomas Linacre, in 1518 when he gave the College use of his own home, known as the Stone House. Located just south of St Paul's Cathedral on Knightrider Street, two rooms were given over to the College as a meeting room and a library. In 1524 Linacre bequeathed the house to the College and a theatre was later added for anatomy lectures.

In 1614 the College leased a house at Amen Corner, Paternoster Row, having outgrown the Stone House. The building was probably modified to provide a meeting room with a library above and also had two rooms for anatomy lectures, as well as accommodation for a resident Fellow. William Harvey donated his personal collections along with funds to build a new library and museum in 1654, but the building and most of its contents were

The College at Amen Corner

The courtyard and Cutlerian Theatre at Warwick Lane

The Long Room, Warwick Lane, by Roulandson and Pugin, in 1808

destroyed in 1666 during the Great Fire of London. The Library Keeper, Christopher Merrett, was able to save legal documents as well as ceremonial items, around 100 books and a portrait of Harvey – still on display in the College Library today.

The College was homeless for nine years following the fire, meeting in Fellows' houses while fundraising for a new building. Finally opening in 1675, the first institutional home was designed by Robert Hooke and situated in Warwick Lane. It was arranged around a courtyard with public rooms occupying the central section and apartment wings for letting to each side. A gift from London merchant and financier Sir John Cutler provided money to build an anatomy theatre with a distinctive octagonal dome, and Fellow Baldwin Hamey financed a grand public gallery known as the Long Room, lined with decorative oak panelling. In 1680, Henry Pierrepont, Marquis of Dorchester, presented his magnificent book collection to the College on the condition that the College would build a suitable library to house it. The collection was installed after Sir Christopher Wren had made the necessary alterations. For the first time, the College had a large and elegant home, which attracted visitors and tourists, but the City location gradually grew less desirable: the diarist John Evelyn wrote that it was a pity the

*The new College of Physicians,
Pall Mall East, by Thomas Barber
after Thomas Hosmer Shepherd,
1828*

College was built 'in so obscure a hole'. Public life and fashionable society were moving west, away from the crowded City, and in 1799 the College decided to follow suit.

The College moved west in 1825 as the architect John Nash was remodelling much of the chosen area. Plans were submitted by Nash for the College, but they were rejected in favour of a design by Robert Smirke in the new Pall Mall East, with windows on one side overlooking what would become Trafalgar Square. Originally the building housed both the physicians and the Union Club and was architecturally similar to many of the gentlemen's clubs of the Pall Mall area. A dominating entrance portico of six Ionic columns led inside to facilities reflecting the College's move away from practical medicine, with no anatomy theatre and no laboratory. From the entrance, a grand staircase led to a double storey library lit by skylights and on the ground floor a dining room doubled as a lecture theatre. The Censors' Room on the first floor was lined with the panelling taken from Warwick Lane. As early as 1920 the College was again considering the suitability of its home as the building was deemed too small. It was sold to the Canadian Embassy in 1963, allowing the opportunity to move to Regent's Park.

Architectural plans

Architectural plans

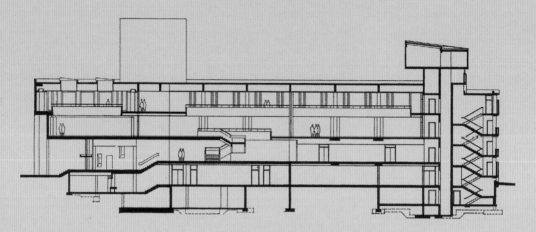

Longitudinal section

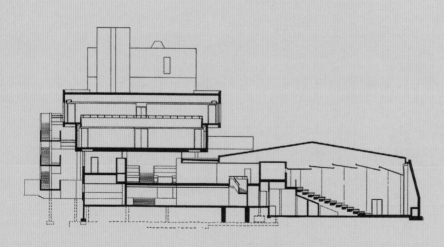

Transversal section

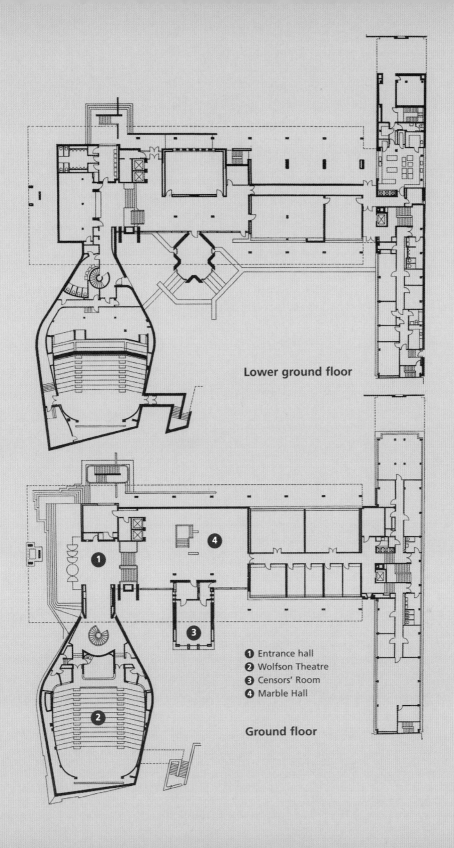

Lower ground floor

Ground floor

1 Entrance hall
2 Wolfson Theatre
3 Censors' Room
4 Marble Hall

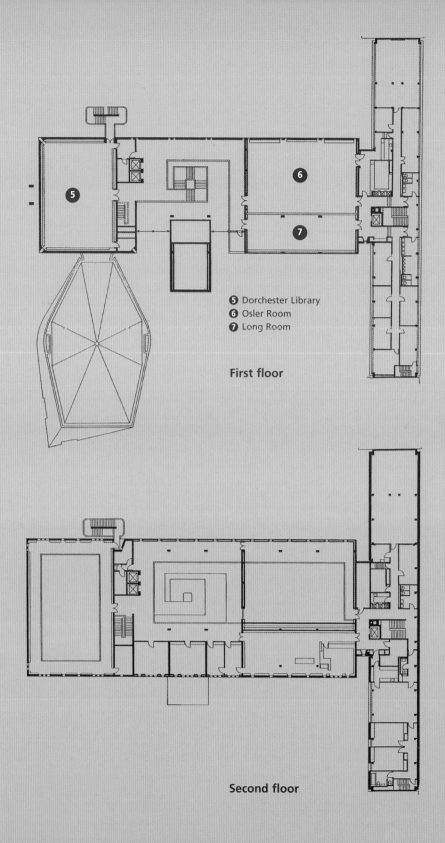

⑤ Dorchester Library
⑥ Osler Room
⑦ Long Room

First floor

Second floor

List of illustrations

Room guide

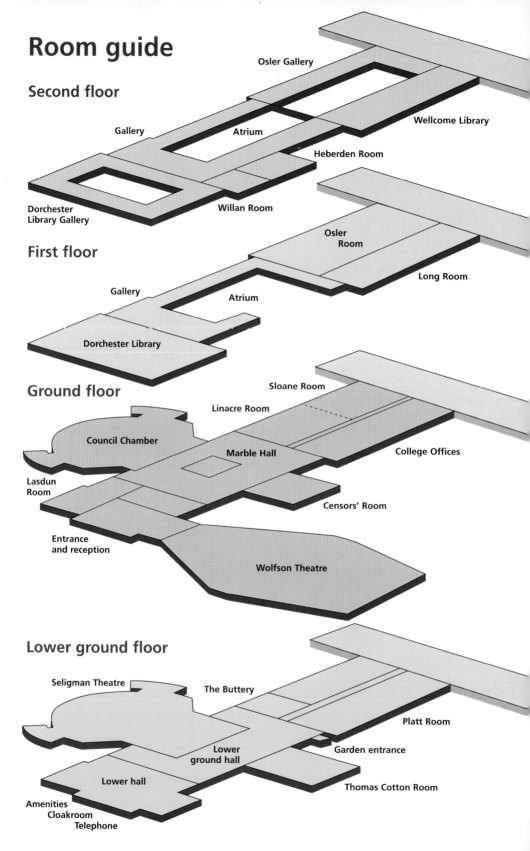

Second floor

Osler Gallery

Wellcome Library

Gallery

Atrium

Heberden Room

Dorchester
Library Gallery

Willan Room

First floor

Osler
Room

Long Room

Gallery

Atrium

Dorchester Library

Ground floor

Sloane Room

Linacre Room

Council Chamber

Marble Hall

College Offices

Lasdun
Room

Censors' Room

Entrance
and reception

Wolfson Theatre

Lower ground floor

Seligman Theatre

The Buttery

Platt Room

Lower
ground hall

Garden entrance

Lower hall

Amenities
Cloakroom
Telephone

Thomas Cotton Room